THE
GOLDEN ISLES

Text
Bill Harris

Captions
Bill Harris

Design
Teddy Hartshorn

Photography
South Stock, Atlanta, Georgia
The Jekyll Island Authority,
Jekyll Island, Georgia

Editorial
David Gibbon

Production
Ruth Arthur
Sally Connolly
Neil Randles
Karen Staff

Director of Production
Gerald Hughes

CLB 2862
© 1993 CLB Publishing Ltd., Godalming, Surrey, England.
All rights reserved.
This 1993 edition published by Crescent Books,
distributed by Outlet Book Company, Inc., a Random House Company,
40 Engelhard Avenue, Avenel, New Jersey 07001
Color separations by Scantrans Pte Ltd., Singapore
Printed and bound in Singapore
ISBN 0 517 07259 9
8 7 6 5 4 3 2 1

THE
GOLDEN ISLES

CRESCENT BOOKS
NEW YORK • AVENEL, NEW JERSEY

Depending on your point of view, General William T. Sherman's Georgia campaign in the Civil War was either one of the greatest military strategies in American history or one of the very worst. But either way, the burning of Atlanta makes most of us forget that Sherman's army was on a "March to the Sea," and that the last stop was Savannah. Once having taken this city, and symbolically given it to his Commander-in-Chief, Abraham Lincoln, as a Christmas gift, he gave the territory between Savannah and the sea to the freed slaves who had followed his army across the state.

It was his intention to create an independent state where blacks could control their own destiny, and his order, which covered "the islands from Charleston south, and the abandoned rice fields along the rivers for thirty miles back from the sea," specifically prohibited any white persons from buying property or living on any of the islands or in coastal settlements. As many as 30,000 blacks marched into Savannah behind Sherman, but thousands more were already in the islands he proposed to give them, where they had been living under the protection of New England missionaries and Union Army soldiers for four years. They were the beneficiaries of the so-called Port Royal Experiment, whose leaders had proclaimed Hilton Head Island the "Promised Land."

The missionaries, who called themselves "Gideonites," arrived in 1861 right behind the Federal Marines, who established a beach-head on the island as the center of a blockade of Southern ports. Their goal, they said, was not only to Christianize the former slaves, but to "elevate them in the scale of humanity." It was true that they had to free some of the local slaves at gunpoint, and that they seemed more interested in growing cotton than food, but they did teach their charges to read, a skill that would be indispensable if Sherman's Black Separatist Empire was to have any chance of success.

As it turned out, the emperor he chose had been educated up North and had been one of the few blacks who went to Hilton Head as a Gideonite. A fiery Abolitionist, Tunis Campbell's life-long dream had been to migrate to Liberia, but he recognized the similarities between Sherman's plan and the West African Republic that had been founded as a haven for freed American slaves, and when he was appointed Governor of the Golden Isles he wasted no time moving down to St. Catherines Island to take charge.

The freedmen who had followed Sherman had been left to starve on the Savannah waterfront and in camps on Hilton Head, and Campbell had no time to waste. But there was plenty of game on St. Catherines and fish on its shores, and as a minister of the Methodist Episcopal Church their governor was able to give them food for the soul and faith in the future. Then he set about to structure that future. He began by writing a constitution, appointing a cabinet and establishing a legislature. He also organized a court and sent to Africa for a judge whose major duty was enforcing Sherman's rule that white men were not welcome in any of the barrier islands. And to back him up, Campbell recruited an army of every able-bodied man on St. Catherines Island. He also dug into his own pocket to import two teachers from New York to make sure his people could get an education. And he provided jobs for them cutting the island's pine trees and selling the lumber.

It seemed like the answer to a beautiful dream, but it turned out to be nothing more than a dream. Not long after the end of the war, land speculators began carving up the islands among themselves, and when they arrived to claim their seaside plantations, Campbell's little army was strained to the limit fighting them off. And when Federal troops were sent in, Campbell was forced to run for his life. His island empire was dissolved, but the world hadn't heard the last of Tunis Campbell. He re-established his people in a burned-out plantation on the mainland, and a year later, after a massive drive to encourage his flock to register to vote, he became a state senator. With that, he established himself and his people in Darien and began rebuilding the Black Separatist Empire. His fellow senators in Atlanta characterized him as an "insolent ape," but Campbell never deviated from his lifelong dedication to black power, which he called "heart power." He fought for, and won, the right of blacks to ride the same streetcars as whites, and he went to Washington to lobby for a bill that eventually outlawed the Ku Klux Klan. When he was ousted from the state legislature on the grounds that giving blacks the right to vote didn't give them the right to hold office, he went off to Washington again and, when the law was changed, he had his job back.

It would be an understatement to say that Campbell was unpopular among the whites along the coast and in the islands. But even after he created an international incident by confiscating foreign ships because of the way their masters treated black crewmen, the courts seemed powerless against him for those and other crimes, both real and imagined. They finally managed to convict him on charges of falsely imprisoning a white man and he was forced to go to prison himself. When he was released he went back north again, and the dream of turning Georgia's Golden Isles into a black empire died then and there. It had lasted only a dozen years.

Tunis Campbell wasn't the first to dream of an empire in the sea islands. The area around Hilton Head became the site of the first Spanish settlement north of the Caribbean in 1526, nearly forty years before the establishment of St. Augustine on the Florida coast. It died when its founder did, but the Spanish didn't lose interest in the islands. When French Huguenots established a colony on Port Royal Sound, the Spaniards drove them out and began exploring the other sea islands, beginning with St. Catherines, where the Indians welcomed them with open arms. Encouraged by the prospect of what seemed to be an endless supply of pearls and a native population apparently willing to become Christians, they established a base on Cumberland Island and began making plans to add the Georgia coast to their Spanish-American Empire.

Over the next hundred years, coastal Georgia became the most important source of food and Indian slave labor for Spain's settlements in Florida. But things began to change in 1663, when England's King Charles II made a gift of the Carolinas to a few of his friends and announced that its southern boundary was in the area of Daytona Beach, well south of the Spanish fortress at St. Augustine. Naturally, the Spanish weren't too pleased, but they were no match for the English traders, who found it quite easy to convince the Indians that the Spanish were their enemies. The combination of native uprisings and pirate raids finally eliminated the Spanish presence, and English adventurers established a feudal colony on the Georgia coast which they called Azila. Its hopeful founder, Sir Robert Montgomery, called the string of islands "The Golden Isles" because of the way they fairly glow in the sunlight, and to add a dash of promotional romance to his barony. His scheme to turn the islands into gardens of silk and olive trees, coffee plantations and almond groves sounded good on paper, but the experiment failed in the face of Indian raids and vengeful Spaniards. The key to success, obviously, was to get more Englishmen interested in providing the safety of numbers.

The first attempts to settle the southern end of the Carolina grant were dismal failures. The earliest to try were New Englanders, who not only found the coast inhospitable, but left a sign on a tree warning off others who might try to re-establish their abandoned colony. But men who had emigrated to Barbados and found themselves unwelcome there organized an expedition headed by Captain William Hilton, to see if they might succeed where others had failed. He landed on the island that he named for himself in 1663 and wrote a glowing report of the area that the Carolina proprietors were pleased to circulate back home in England. Referring to the "scandalous writing" left behind by the New Englanders, Hilton said he had found the land as good any he had ever seen, and that it was "sufficient to accommodate thousands of our English nation." The promotion didn't stir many in the English nation itself, but in 1670 the Barbadians landed a bedraggled group in Port Royal. They didn't stay long because of the Spanish threat, but moved up the coast and settled in a place they called Charles Town. The Golden Isles didn't figure in any Englishman's plans for another sixty years.

Compared to all the others that had come and gone, it was a quite unusual plan. It began in 1728, when James Oglethorpe used his position as a member of Parliament to reform English prisons. It was an idea whose time had come, but it raised the new problem of what to do with all those former prisoners. The answer, said Oglethorpe, was to create a colony for them in America. It made perfect sense. Not only would these people produce crops the mother country needed, but their presence would help keep the Spanish in their place. Oglethorpe and his partners also reasoned that bringing Christianity to the Indians was reason enough to establish a new colony, and when they suggested naming it for King George II, their request was granted.

Oglethorpe himself arrived in Georgia with the first colonists in 1733 and began building the city of

Savannah. He also negotiated with the Creek Indians for the land around his new town and secured possession of St. Simons, Cumberland and Amelia Islands, along with Sea Island and Jekyll, reserving St. Catherines, Ossabaw and Sapelo as Indian hunting grounds. The islands were important to him because of his promise to keep the Spaniards from encroaching on English territory, and he wasted no time establishing a presence on St. Simons by building the town of Frederica, which included what he characterized as "a pretty strong fort." He put a second fort at another point on the island and sited cannon emplacements at the southern end of Cumberland Island. And between them, on Jekyll Island, he built a brewery to keep the troops happy. Oglethorpe had passed a law prohibiting rum, brandy and other "spirits or strong waters" from his colony, but he thought that fine wine and "good English beer and ale" would make his people stronger.

Their strength was tested in 1742, when a Spanish fleet sailed north and anchored in Jekyll Sound with their cannon aimed at Fort St. Simons. The Governor responded by dismantling his battery and retreating to Frederica. The Spaniards had brought 5,000 troops, but the Georgians had only 700 men, and to make matters worse their supply line to the mainland was cut off. But James Oglethorpe wasn't without resources. When he learned that one of his men had defected to the other side, the Governor wrote a fanciful note to him, saying that he was expecting a fleet of British ships and a regiment of reinforcements, and asking him to keep talking until the help arrived. As Oglethorpe had hoped, the Spanish intercepted the note and, assuming the defector was a spy, moved their ships out of range and left their soldiers on the island to fend for themselves. When the troops began marching in the direction of Frederica, Oglethorpe personally led a charge into their ranks and, as they turned and ran, he stationed men behind trees to keep them from coming back. Spanish losses were slight, even though the encounter was called the Battle of Bloody Marsh, but Oglethorpe managed to demoralize the enemy completely, and a few days later the Spanish were gone. They never came back.

Oglethorpe himself left Georgia for the last time soon afterward. The colony's English trustees had long since become disenchanted with him and had sent a new man, William Stephens, to take over. His first act was to divide the colony into two counties, leaving Oglethorpe in control of the southern district. For his part, the founder of Savannah said he was perfectly happy to be exiled to Frederica. He said the islands were much healthier anyway, and when he made his final exit he didn't bother to travel up to Savannah for a last goodbye.

When James Oglethorpe declared the sea islands "healthy" most people dismissed the claim as sour grapes. But in the 1880s a group of the richest men in America challenged a team of doctors to find the healthiest place in the world to build a retreat. Money was no object, and the medics combed the coast from Maine to Florida, even traveling to Europe to have a look at the French Riviera before reaching the conclusion that Oglethorpe had the right idea, and that the Golden Isles were the perfect choice. The doctors didn't say which of the islands was best, but by what may or may not be a coincidence, John Du Bignon, whose ancestors had established a sea island cotton plantation on Jekyll Island, had just bought the whole island for $13,000 and he was willing to sell. One hundred of the richest men in the country, including William K. Vanderbilt, J.P. Morgan and Vincent Astor, combined to pay him $125,000 for his island and then hired a landscape architect to transform it into a "winter Newport" they called the Jekyll Island Club.

Unlike Newport, their clubhouse and the mansions built by individual members were carefully designed to make a simple statement. Nothing gaudy was to be permitted, but if simplicity was the watchword, every effort was made to build something substantial, even if their owners did call them "cottages." Such architects as the firm of Carrere and Hastings, who had designed a New York mansion for Henry Clay Frick, and John Russell Pope, whose later credits include Washington's National Gallery and the Jefferson Memorial, contributed to the island's ambiance. The forests were stocked with pheasants and wild boar brought from Italy, but outsiders of the human variety were admitted by invitation only, and even such invited guests as Winston Churchill and President William McKinley were reminded that they really didn't "belong" on Jekyll Island.

The Club's golden age came to an abrupt end in 1942, when a German submarine was spotted just off the Georgia coast. A concerned President Roosevelt dispatched General George S. Patton to evacuate the island of its vulnerable millionaires, and he was forceful enough to close down the Jekyll Island Club virtually overnight. Its officers planned to reopen after the war, but in 1947 the island was sold to become a state park. A causeway was built to connect Jekyll to the mainland and, in the years since, many of the irreplaceable buildings have been restored. The beaches, marshes and woodlands have been protected and, in addition to a convention center, ten hotels and resorts have been added. But even with golf courses and tennis centers and a huge theme park that includes a swimming pool with simulated ocean waves, the island is still every bit the natural paradise the medical men preferred over the French Riviera a century ago.

All of the Golden Isles are remarkably free of reminders of twentieth-century progress. Cumberland, the biggest on the Georgia coast, became protected as a National Seashore in 1972, and there isn't a restaurant or gift shop anywhere along its sixteen-mile length of clean white sand fringing the Atlantic Ocean. Its western side is a salt marsh and its interior a forest of live oak trees filled with wildlife and flocks of seabirds. The only roads have been reduced to footpaths leading to the remnants of such landmarks as the first Spanish Jesuit mission in what is now the United States, and Dungeness, the plantation where Eli Whitney introduced his cotton gin.

The modern world arrived at Hilton Head in 1956, when lumberman Fred Hack decided to stop cutting trees and start building a resort. But his idea for Sea Pines Plantation wasn't in the mold of other seaside developments. He didn't want any electric signs or billboards; highrise buildings were forbidden in the neighborhood and the homes he built were all elegant but understated, and designed to blend in with the dunes and woodland. He hired a Japanese landscape architect to set the stage, and together they created a planned community whose ideas have been followed all over the country. But back in the fifties there wasn't a resort builder anywhere who didn't think Fred Hack had made a very expensive mistake. Of course, they were wrong: Hilton Head hasn't stopped growing since. The original Sea Pines covers 5,700 acres, ten percent of which is a forested wildlife preserve, but there is more to Hilton Head Island than the Sea Pines Resort. The island has twelve miles of beaches and twenty-five miles of bicycle paths winding through three nature preserves. It has 23 golf courses, 300 tennis courts, 30 shopping centers, 100 restaurants, 2,000 hotel rooms and more than 4,000 houses and condos for rent. It has its own airport, seven marinas and a bridge connecting it to the mainland. But after more than forty years, there still isn't a billboard anywhere on Hilton Head Island, and if you need directions to a praline store or feel the need to take home a chenille bedspread, you'll have to drive back across the bridge. Neither Hilton Head nor any of the Golden Isles are the place to find such pleasures. On the other hand, if your taste runs to clean air and water, marshes alive with wildlife, skies filled with birds, and beaches where you can walk for hours without stumbling over blankets and picnic baskets, it's all out there on those beautiful islands. If your taste runs to history, it's there, too, in the ghostly ruins of old forts and plantations and in abandoned burial grounds where, according to tradition, the spirits of the dead appear by day and not by night as in other places. And when they do, they are bathed in light – golden light.

Part of the fun at Hilton Head Island can be found at the 18th hole at Broad Creek Golf Course (above left), around the statue of Neptune (above) at Shelter Cove Marina, and by the lighthouse at Sea Pines Plantation Marina (facing page top). A quiet beginning to an active day on one of Hilton Head's beaches (facing page bottom) contrasts with the opening ceremony of the island's annual Heritage Golf Tournament (below). Below left: Melrose Plantation Golf Course, one of twenty-three to choose from on this island, and (left) shrimp boats gearing up for a day's work and a well-earned and tasty dinner tonight.

The sun is one of Hilton Head's biggest attractions, and it keeps on adding to the island's pleasure right up until the last minute of the day (overleaf), when its final rays silhouette the trees (left), provide a backdrop for romantic strolls along the beach (bottom left), and light the way for shore birds looking for that last tasty morsel at the water's edge (center left). And when night finally comes to Sea Pines Plantation harbor and lighthouse (below) the pleasure doesn't end, it just becomes something different in the festive glow of thousands of twinkling lights.

Wassaw Island (facing page, above and below) is the most primitive of the Georgia sea islands. As a national wildlife sanctuary, its marshes and virgin forests are off-limits to the public. Its nearest neighbor, Skidaway Island (right) is the site of a state park. Also nearby, to Wassaw's north, is Tybee Island (above right, below right and overleaf), where Georgia's founder, James Oglethorpe, first set foot in the New World in 1733. Tybee is one of the state's oldest resorts.

20

The best time to visit the old timber port of Darien, which lies just north of St. Simons Island, is during the first week in April for the annual blessing of the shrimp fleet (facing page). Shrimp boats (below), as well as their catch, are an important part of the sea island scene.

Above left: a relic of the past overlooking a Sapelo Island salt marsh and (above) another, the ruins of "Chocolate," the castle on Sapelo Island that was built by the Marquis de Montelet. Facing page: (top) the intercoastal waterway flowing past St. Catherines Island on its way from New England to Florida, and (bottom) Cabretta Beach, one of Sapelo's protected delights. Below: Sapelo Island Light, once useful to ships bound for Darien, (below left) St. Catherine's west shore, and (left) the unusual turkey fountain at the Sapelo Island Marine Institute, a center of marsh research. The Sapelo Light (overleaf) has been fighting a gallant battle with beach erosion since it was built in 1820.

Above left: rare wood storks roosting on Little St. Simons Island, (above) part of Little St. Simons virgin forest, and (facing page) exploring Sea Island the old-fashioned way. Below: art of the moment – some impressive sand sculptures on a St. Simons beach, and (below left) nature's own version of sand sculptures: sand dunes are an ever-shifting gallery of beauty. Left: a sand dollar seashell spent by the action of the waves. By the time the sun sets on St. Simons Island (overleaf), the beach won't look quite the same as it did this morning, and tomorrow it will change again.

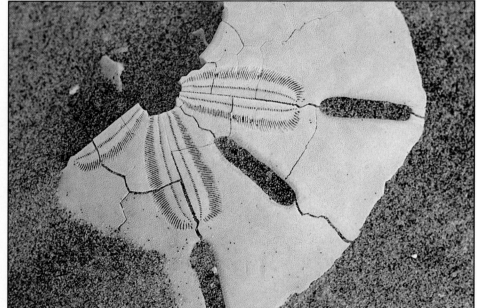

A natural paradise, the Golden Isles are a perfect retreat for fishing (above left); honeymooning at Sea Island's Cloister resort (above); being treated like royalty at the King & Prince Hotel (facing page top) on St. Simons Island; or simply watching the sun go down on a St. Simons pier (facing page bottom). St. Simons is also the ideal place for catching up with history as a costumed park ranger (below) molds musket balls at Fort Frederica, while Frederica's historic Christ Church (below left) is also interesting. Left: a salt marsh at low tide on St. Simons Island, and (overleaf) one of America's most elegant resorts, the Cloister on Sea Island, the perfect holiday base.

A beach can be the source of all kinds of pleasure, whether it is a volleyball game (facing page top), a destination for a catamaran cruise (below), or a quiet place to be dazzled by the sun (facing page bottom).

Jekyll Island (these pages) is the smallest of the Golden Isles, but it is big on natural resources, abounding in deer, turkey and quail, as well as thousands of shorebirds, English pheasants and wild boar, introduced for the pleasure of hunters. Its marshes and forests, tidal creeks and windswept beaches have hardly changed in appearance since they formed the favorite offshore hunting grounds of the Creek Indians. The island became a refuge for French Huguenots in 1562 and Spanish Jesuits four years later. It was a cotton plantation before becoming a playground for the rich in the 1880s.

The Jekyll Island Club (below and overleaf), now a hotel, was once the playground of millionaires, such as J.P. Morgan and the Vanderbilts, many of whom lived in elaborate "cottages." The 1892 Rockefeller mansion Indian Mound (facing page) is one such luxury dwelling.

There is never a dull moment on Jekyll Island, where golfers find challenges through woodlands and marshlands on the Oleander Course (above left and below) or the nine-hole Oceanside (above), built in 1898 for the original residents of the millionaires' village. The action never seems to stop at the thirteen clay courts of the island's Tennis Center (left and facing page), and for quieter pleasures there are twenty miles of wooded bike trails (below left) that are ideal for exploring the island. But the main event for many is Frantic Atlantic (overleaf), a 180-foot swimming pool whose water is churned into four-foot-high waves at the aptly named Summer Waves park.

47

The Jekyll Island Marina (below and right) was built as a ferry slip and dock for members of the Jekyll Island Club. J.P. Morgan's yacht Corsair, named for the ship used by his ancestor, the buccaneer Sir Henry Morgan, was frequently tied up here. After the club closed in the 1940s, DuBignon Cottage (center right) was abandoned until 1989, when it was restored and refurnished with items from the collection of the Jekyll Island Museum. The most imposing of the island's homes is the Crane Cottage (bottom right), built for the plumbing manufacturer Richard T. Crane, Jr. Its Mediterranean style was considered too ostentatious when it was built in 1916. But though the millionaires of the Jekyll Island Club couldn't resist enhancing the place, they left most of the island, including ten miles of wide beaches (overleaf), virtually the same as they found it.

Cumberland Island (these pages and overleaf), the southernmost of the Golden Isles, is a National Seashore and one of the last unspoiled beaches in America. Its wildlife ranges from alligators and deer to raccoons and mink – and the occasional human visitors who take the forty-five-minute ferry ride out from St. Mary's for a few days of camping. Cumberland's fauna also includes fine wild horses believed to be descended from Spanish mounts, as well as a population of mules whose ancestors were imported from Sicily. The island is a favorite nesting ground for birds of every description, from marsh wrens to pelicans, storks and other spectacular water birds.

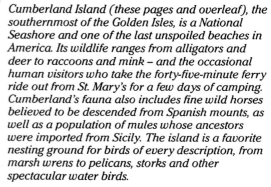

Although Cumberland Island is forever wild, and filled with huge live oaks (right), there are still many traces of human history in such sites as Plum Orchard (below), a now-abandoned estate built in 1900 for George Carnegie. Dungeness Mansion (center right), originally the home of Revolutionary War hero Nathaniel Greene and once called the most elegant residence on the coast, was burned not long after the Civil War, leaving the charred remains of its six-foot walls. Greyfield Inn (bottom right) was built by the descendants of the millionaire Thomas Carnegie and his wife, Lucy, who bought Cumberland Island after reading about it in a magazine in 1880. The island, which James Oglethorpe maintained as a hunting preserve in colonial days, has been administered by the National Park Service since 1972.

There are nearly twenty organized campsites on Cumberland Island, as well as a few primitive back-country sites. The year-round ferry that takes campers from the fishing port at St. Mary's (above and last page) drops them at the island's only dock (facing page, below and below right) in plenty of time to catch the sunset through the festoons of Spanish moss at Brickhill Bluff (above right) and to watch the sunrise on the twenty-mile-long beach (right and overleaf).